After the Ball
Breda Sullivan

Salmonpoetry

Published in 1998 by
Salmon Publishing Ltd,
Cliffs of Moher, Co. Clare

A catalogue record for this book is available from the British Library.

The Arts Council   Salmon Publishing gratefully acknowledges the
An Chomhairle Ealaíon   financial assistance of The Arts Council.

ISBN 1 897648 21 9 Softcover
ISBN 1 897648 33 2 Hardcover

Cover illustration by Austin Carey
Cover design by Brenda Dermody
Set by Siobhán Hutson
Printed by Betaprint, Clonshaugh, Dublin 17

In memory of my parents
Anne Troy and Patrick Ducke

and for Basil,
Barry, Troy, Eimear and Declan
with love

Acknowledgements

Acknowledgements are due to the editors of the following in which some of the poems in this collection first appeared:

Journals: *The Frogmore Papers* (UK); *Figments*; *Cyphers*; *Waterford Review*; *Books Ireland*; *Force 10*; *Education Today*; *Riposte*; *Honest Ulsterman*; *Poetry Ireland Review*; *Cúirt Journal*; *The Edgeworth Papers*; *Other Poetry* (UK); *Madame Bulls Tavern* (Canada); *Writing in the West* (Connacht Tribune); *The Longford Leader*; *The Longford News*.

Anthologies: *Rainbows and Stone*; *Women's Work Anthologies*; *Six for Gold*; *Beneath the Moat II*; *Belfast Still Dreamin'*.

A special thanks to fellow poet Aine Miller for her invaluable advice.

Contents

I

Bone   3
The Inspection   4
Simple Addition   5
What I Remember ...   16
After the Ball   17
Snow Feathers   18
Rest in Peace   19
The Parish Dance   20

II

Anchor   23
The Homecoming   24
Looking Back   25
Rubber Gloves   26
Empathy   27
Between   28
Winter Sequence   29

III

Fionnuala's Song   35
Birth   36
Cathal   37
Child in a Bottle   38
Black Briars   39
First Steps   40
A Child Kneeling   42

IV

Coolnagun Bog	45
Middle Age	46
Salt	47
Armchair Travel	48
A Black Dog Sleeps	49
A Line of Washing	50
Mirror Mirror	51
Famine	52
Retirement	53
Midsummer Night	54

I

Bone

I dust the blackboard now and think of bone
strong bone disintegrating into dust
white powder on the cold grey flags of stone.

My mother broke her hip, I heard her groan
the ambulance arrived and no one fussed
I dust the blackboard now and think of bone.

At the clinic for the screening of the bone
I check in, wait my turn, I think of rust
and powder on the cold grey flags of stone.

Back forth, back forth, back forth the scanner zone
I lie, stare ceiling-wards, I do not trust
I dust the blackboard now and think of bone.

The gene that wrecked her hip betrays my bone
already the destruction is like lust
white powder on the cold grey flags of stone.

I walk, drink milk, eat yogurt and I moan
my bone a honeycomb, this is not just.
I dust the blackboard now and think of bone
white powder on the cold grey flags of stone.

The Inspection

A social worker
calling
to our house
would find
no dust
under our beds,
in the cupboard
all the linen
gleaming white,
all our meals
nourishing,
all bread and cakes
home-made.

On a winter's day
warm coats, caps,
scarves and mitts
insulated us
against the cold.

If she fine-combed
my fair waist-length hair
she would find
nothing,
no sign
of a child
locked for hours
in a dark place,
nor would she see
on the ceiling of my mind
the hair-cracks.

Simple Addition

i

In the silence
after thunder
I return
slide the latch
in the small iron gate
my feet remember
the short concrete path
the door opens
before I ring the bell
the smell of Sunday roast
whispering in the oven
the table set
white cloth
gleaming cutlery and delph
the fire flickers
warm in the hearth
while on the sideboard
pale petals drip
from a bowl of roses.

ii

Between the flash
and the growl of thunder
a woman and four children
huddled under a table
praying the rosary
for his safe return.
Between the flash
and the growl of thunder
I still hear
his key turn.

5

iii
When we heard
a donkey bray
away over the bog
he took off his hat
held it to his chest
blessed himself and said
tonight some poor travelling man
will meet his end.

When we saw
a star fall
from a frosty sky
she held
my gloved hand tight
blessed herself and said
some poor soul has died
and is gone to God.

iv
My father carrying my bag
holding my hand
I snailing along

we were late
the hall was empty
he knocked at a door

a voice said 'Tar isteach'
and we stepped in
to staring eyes and a nun

he gave her my bag
tucked a clean hankie up my sleeve
I started to cry ....

v

If she wasn't sitting in her chair
by the gleaming black range

drinking a cup of tea listening
to 'Mrs. Dale's Diary' on BBC

clouds stormed the horizon
thunder grumbled

in the breath-held silence
I counted ....

vi

The doorbell ringing
and she rushing
to the sink with
Don't open it yet
don't open it yet
dipping in a glass jar
for her false teeth
rinsing them under the tap
turning her back
drying her fingers
on her crossover bib
then with a false smile saying
You can open it now.

vii

On the dot of six thirty
the front door clicks softly shut.

I picture her
hurrying by dark houses

over Battery Bridge
and the canal

past the unlit shops
of Connaught St. and Pearse St.

across the Bridge
of Athlone.

I cover my head as the river wind
nibbles her ears, her face.

Halfway up Church St. she turns right,
down the steep, narrow lane to the Friary.

Inside it is warm and bright.
Always she kneels by the side altar

in the second seat close
to the rails for receiving.

I force myself to stay awake
until Mass is half over

shiver out of bed tiptoe
on cold lino to the warming kitchen.

I lift the lid off the range
feed sod after sod of turf

to the dying embers
kindled by her numb fingers.

I slide the lukewarm kettle
closer to the heat.

Back in bed I curl, a frozen ball
and soon I am sleeping

knowing that when her key turns
the fire will glow for her, the kettle sing.

viii
My mother coming up the stairs
on frosty nights

opening the wardrobe wide
removing my father's overcoat

placing it on the bed
over blankets and eiderdown.

Her eau-de-cologne lingers
and from his coat

a faint scent of camphor
of must.

ix
Coats ending
above the knees

gartered socks reaching
to the knees

and the raw cold
in between.

x
She warmed
the bottle
of olive oil
in a saucepan
in a corner
of the range
tested it
on the inside
of her wrist
sat in her chair.

I knelt
before her
placed my head
in her lap
the surprise of warmth
a faint smell
of red soap
from her navy
cross-over.

A trickle
of olive oil
in my ear.

xi
I am lonely
for floral oil-cloth
on a square table,
the black kettle
hissing on the range,
the smell
of griddle bread,
the feel
of a leather school-bag,
four heads bent
over four copies
and four pencils
busy doing sums.

xii
Every evening
big brother and I
crossed the road
walked down
the hilly lane
for the milk
he carried
the big can
and I the small one
with the lid
and we planned

he would be
a parish priest
with a big house
and a car
shiny, black
and he would let me
be his housekeeper.

xiii
If I dawdled
the gang waited.

If I hurried
they caught up.

Surrounded me chanting
'We heard your mother

and father fighting
again last night.'

The walls of our house
collapsed. On the floor

the green enamel teapot
in a puddle of steaming tea

the dent where it hit
the wall exposed.

xiv
I am listening
to hear a key
turn in a lock
to know my father
is home from work
behind his back
a brown paper bag
full of grapes.

xv
I peel a reed
in a heather sea

while he turns turf
on the high bank.

xvi
I sat
on my father's coat
on a load of turf

he shook the reins
clicked his tongue
the donkey started for home

on my bumpy throne
down the long bog road
I was queen of the world.

xvii
On Friday evening
after tea
when the table
was cleared
the dishes washed
and put away
he sat one end
of the table
a cylinder of pennies
on the oil-cloth
before him.

We stood in a line
youngest first
eldest last
one by one
we said our age
and he paid us
our weekly wage
a big brown penny
for every year
that had passed.

xviii
Up and down
the back road
his lopsided walk
aided with a stick
his left arm
a V across his chest
his helpless hand
gathered under his chin.

I knelt before him
put on his warm lined boots
lifted each leg
placed each foot
on the wheelchair step
his hand on my head
a benediction.

xix
At sixteen
waiting on tables
washing dishes
drying dishes
sweeping floors
mopping floors

scrubbing floors
cleaning toilets
burning sanitary towels
making ice-cream cones
from ten in the morning
until midnight
six days a week
for two pounds.

And Friday tea-time
meeting her
outside Lipton's
handing her
the brown envelope
and she hurrying
to get the groceries
before the shop closed.

What I Remember …

is a baby
lying crosswise
on the bed

my aunt's face
damp
when I kissed her

a hackney cab
my uncle in the back
the white box on his lap

the midwife burying
baby clothes
in earth and ashes.

When she was gone
my mother dug them up
rinsed them in the sink

hung them on the line
saying waste
was a sin

and please God
they would be needed
again.

After the Ball

The sudden loneliness you feel
when the band plays
after the ball
and you are drowning
in a sea
of swaying bodies
waving arms
while in a kitchen
a child
watches a woman
stir tea-cloths
boiling on the range
scrub sheets white
on a wash-board
in the sink
her strong arms
bangled with suds
and all the while she sings
after the ball is over
after the break of morn
and later in the garden
you hand her pegs
until she hoists her line
of dazzling white
to the sunny wind
a sheet slaps
a sudden shower
on your upturned face
and when you climb the steps
to the back door
behind you
she is humming still.

Snow Feathers

A flurry of snowflakes
beyond the red candle
in my window

a flurry of black feathers
from the turkey my father plucked
so many Christmas Eves ago

I watch white feathers
sail
in an opaque sky

while outside the back door
on a kitchen chair
my father sits

his feet
buried
in black snow.

Rest in Peace

My bare hands scrabbled
the black earth
clay clogged nails
dug furiously
like a famished dog
frantic for a bone.

Your skeleton white
in the black hole.

I climbed in
lay beside you
my touch
collapsed your ribs
I bundled
all your bones
hugged them tightly to me
kissed your leering skull.

I found the hand
that held me safe
through childhood.

I hold it still.

The Parish Dance

I went to the parish dance
in the Park House
a week after I buried my mother
(just to support it you know)
swore before I left home
I would not set a toe on the floor
just nibble a bit of supper with decorum.

Instead I cleared the plate
and two desserts
heady with white wine
I never left the floor
pausing only in my abandon
to shake the hand
of another neighbour

sorry for my trouble.
Tonight again the parish dances
I stay at home
while my mother
thistledowns from her coffin
and waltzes
barefoot as a blue breeze.

II

Anchor

We moved house
ten times
before I was twenty

since then I have lived
in one house
with one man

sometimes I long to empty cupboards
wrap cups in newspaper
pack them into tea-chests

until I hear
the familiar click
of a door close.

The Homecoming

When I step from the bus
don't stay waiting in the car
and when I sit
into the passenger seat
don't switch on the ignition, indicate,
negotiate the traffic as you tell me
who died while I was away
and the trouble you had saving the hay.

Stand by the bus stop
and wait for me
let the first thing I see
be the blue of your eyes
let me step from the bus
into my home in your arms
the only news
how you missed me.

Looking Back

i.m. James Sullivan

He struggled with the crossword
all day. When evening came
he gave in, asked for help.

It was complete
but for one long word
r-t-o-p-c-i-n.

And the clue?
The undoing
of Lot's wife?

I thought of her
looking back –
retrospection.

With glee he filled in
the final letters
laid down his paper and pen.

He was asleep in seconds
I eased off his glasses
placed them in their case.

Decades later
here I am
Lot's wife.

Rubber Gloves

I was weeding the garden
when my neighbour advised
across the fence
you should wear rubber gloves
when you're doing jobs like that.

I want to feel
the breeze cool my hot hands
leaves and petals kiss my skin
clay clog my fingernails
and the nettle's sting.

Empathy

All day the cow called
for her weaned calf.

The call followed me about the house
while I made beds, hoovered, peeled potatoes.

My small daughter came in the back door.
'The cow is screaming,' she said.

'Cows don't scream,' her brother jeered.
Her two arms hugging her new school-bag,

she listened.
'She's screaming,' I said.

Between

Sitting on a rock
he pulled off
his boots, his socks
tucked a sock
into each boot
placed them on the rock
rolled up each trouser leg
flung the coat
of his Sunday suit
over his shoulder
then, in shirt sleeves and braces
he walked the edge of the Atlantic
his bald head
protected from the sun
by his white handkerchief
knotted at each corner.

Sitting on the same rock
I watch his grand-children
make sand-castles
their father, in T-shirt and shorts
walks the edge of the Atlantic
the day is hot, technicolour
but I am caught
between two times
looking out at
my husband, my children
looking in on
my father
in white shirt sleeves and braces
his black boots
beside me
on the rock.

Winter Sequence

i

I hang a lace curtain
on the corner window
in my living room.

Beyond the lace
winter comes and settles
in my garden.

I do not see
bare branches contort,
the black cat stalk the robin.

In lace light
I read, write overdue letters
knit pink mittens.

Lifting the lace
to see snowflakes
the silent moon.

ii

Where I live
there are no street lights

no frosted pavements
glittering

no next-door neighbour
poking the fire

or in the house
on the other side

no child running
up and down the stairs

where I live
there are no street lights

nothing but a bungalow
like a shoebox

upside-down
in the dark.

iii
The distant lights
of Boherquill

two yellow blobs
on a black canvas

the only evidence
I exist

in the dark
of this rural night.

iv
I have grown fond
of this darkness.

Darkness that covers me
like a sheet.

Sheet of black silk
on white skin.

v
On the shortest day of the year
our cow calved

a day too dense with rain cloud
for a dawn display at Newgrange.

Four o'clock. Shadows gather
outside my window.

I close my eyes
and see

the calf slither into the dark dawn
like a beacon.

vi
I have stayed too long
in midwinter.

Walked on earth
hard as concrete.

Gazed on branches
bare as bone.

Listened
to silent birds.

Shivered
in chill winds.

Closed
the curtains early.

vii
When the first star settles
on my forsythia
I stand on a chair
unhook the lace curtain
from my corner window.

Daffodils thrust through lawn
fisted buds on the hedgerow
unclench a little
catkins dangle from the hazel
a rook wings a twig to the beech.

Spring light floods my living room.
Even the dust dances.

III

Fionnuala's Song

I spread my arms
and they are wings again

huddled on a rock
I see three swans

I battle with the wind
glide down

fold my wings about them
hold them close against the cold

sing softly of our home
near Derravaragh's shore

at last they cease their shivering
and my three brothers sleep

I try to shift my feet
but the frost solders them to the rock

another three hundred years
stretch before us

long and dark
as Aoife's shadow.

Birth

This is the time
my mother-in-law
would light the candle
pace the kitchen floor
her beads worrying
through her fingers.

I stand in the yard
watching my daughter
drag an old milk crate
into an empty stall
from this step
a grand-stand view

over the adjoining wall
the frantic click
of a calving jack
muscles strain
the calf lies limp
in the sun-bright yard.

This is the time
my mother-in-law
would light the candle
pace the kitchen floor
her beads worrying
through her fingers.

Cathal

He lit
eight candles
that Sunday
after Mass in Australia

one for each of his parents
his brothers, his sisters
and last of all
his grandmother

on Monday
he went to work
and the earth shifted
and the digger toppled.

On a Longford farm
his father
trims hedges
before the winter comes

his mother
stays about the house
not wanting to miss
his call from Sydney

in the local
garda station
the phone
rings.

Child in a Bottle

The woman
stood on a chair
reached behind
old paint tins
on a shelf
her fingers closed
on the bottle

the child
came home from school
to the breakfast things
still on the kitchen table

she stood
in the living-room doorway
listening to her mother snore
watching the empty bottle
in her arms
where she longed to be

she closed her eyes
Aliced herself small
crawled inside the bottle

now when her own daughter
toddles to her knee
tugs at her skirt
and dribbles 'Mama, Mama'
she longs to reach out
lift her, hold her
but hesitates, dreading
the cold touch of glass.

Black Briars

She pulled
the trigger

the earth
stood

waves
stayed

gulls
suspended

a puppy
froze

all traffic lights
red

over the window sill
black briars creep

sneak
up the pane.

First Steps

when her children
had gone to school
and her husband
down the field
to count cattle
she tiptoed
to the bedroom
picked up
the plumpest pillow
carried it gently
to the window
sat in her nursing chair
hugged it

new baby smell
his softness
against her cheek
all his perfect
fingers and toes
she remembered
his first pair of shoes
brown with a T strap
and how the others laughed
that first time
he wobbled out the door

the splash she never heard
startled her
from where she sat
the sun played on the river
at the end of the lane
the young mother

dropped an armful of turf
ran into the lane calling
her youngest child by name

all night
she sat by the range
frantic torch beams
spotlighting
every scurrying fear

after midnight
he was carried in
small
she reached for him
blue
she held him
cold
she cuddled him
wet
she kissed him
stiff
she loved him

she cradled the pillow
back to bed
wandered to the kitchen
opened a drawer
took out brown polish, a brush
spread newspaper
one end of the table
and polished
his first pair of shoes
brown with a T strap

A Child Kneeling

A ladybird
drop of blood
lit cigarette
kaleidoscoped
in my lap
startled
I brushed away
nothing
from my green skirt

not even

a child kneeling
on a grassy hill
absorbed in a ladybird
dotting
her white summer skirt

black boots trample daisies

a flicked cigarette arcs the blue sky
his shadow falls on the child.

IV

Coolnagun Bog

The bulldozers are in the bog today
destroying heather, lichen, furze and moss.
While walking down Coole Hill I see the loss
of purple panorama. Far away
the wide horizon, Derravaragh Lake
(where once white feathers were the daily cross)
now blurred from view. Peat powder the new boss,
it peaks in mountains, spews into the air.

Old Phil Doran says developers will go
and this brown desert will become a marsh
and future generations will not know
the spring of turf like carpet, nor the glow
of Summer harvest in the Winter hearth,
the song of lark, bog cotton – globs of snow.

Middle Age

Some women
bake bread
wait for the bingo bus
make patchwork quilts
arrange flowers
paint a landscape
go to assertiveness class
learn computer skills
return to college
study for a degree.

In the fading light
I trawl the skies.

Salt

I asked my father why
the sea was salt.

He pointed
to the hills
across the bay
told me
they were made of salt
and every day
the waves washed
some of the salt away.

In my classroom
teaching a geography lesson
I tell the children
of rivers rushing minerals
to the sea
knowing
of a wide white strand
and the long sea tongues licking.

Armchair Travel

My Granny never saw the sea
her birth, death and in between
a midlander.

We listened in our precious shell
to the swish of ebb and swell
but Granny was deaf.

We brought the sea to her instead
in two brown cider bottles filled
to the brim

With waves where sunstars play
and wild white horses race
for Granny.

In an old tin basin by her own fireside
my Granny paddled in the Atlantic wide
though she never saw the sea.

A Black Dog Sleeps

I sit on a blue step
on the side of a steep hill
the house behind me.

Nasturtium grow in an earthen pot
they spill orange and green
about the blue step.

A child in a red and white shirt
offers me a cookie
from a jar.

In the dusty lane
up the hill
fuchsia bleeds.

A *Line of Washing*

Her head exploded

above her line of washing
a multi-coloured cloud
mushroomed and spread
showered on her back lawn
thousands of coloured plastic letters.
Her children squealed in delight,
played about as in a ball pool,
helped her gather them inside until
every box, cupboard, drawer, bath,
basin, saucepan, bed was filled.
Try as she might
she made no word from them
no story
no poem.

Mirror Mirror

I look in the mirror now
and see
a rose fading

another petal
drips
to the floor

in my daughter's room
slowly
a bud opens

at last
I understand
fairy tales.

Famine

I was born one hundred years
after the great famine

at school I thought
it was all so long ago

now early frost
has touched the crop

I smell the blight
as the black spuds are dug

feel fear and hunger
grip my gut

see my mouth
stained green.

Retirement

I would like to retire
to a small house in Athlone

I would like my brothers and sister
to retire there too

every morning we would waken
to poking and raking in the grate

and then the clink
of cup on saucer

as our father took our mother
her early morning cup of tea

later we would hear cupboard creak
and pot and kettle stir on the range

before the handle of her brush
tapped the ceiling

I would be up
and dressed

opening the kitchen door
I would see

six bowls of porridge
on the table

and six wisps of steam
rise.

Midsummer Night

If I could take
the hem
of this day
pin it to the ground
around the boundary
of my garden
I could dwell forever
in a tent of light
and on midwinter night
wander my garden
before sleep
bathe my face
in bright balmy air
never looking
beyond the hedge
or the fence.

W/D